CONNECT THE NETWORK TO THE NEW NORMAL

FIVE WAYS TO STRENGTHEN MULTI-VOCATIONAL LEADERS

BY CHRIS REINOLDS

Connect the Network to the New Normal: Five Ways to Strengthen Multi-Vocational Leaders by Christopher Reinolds

Published by © The Reinolds Group

Columbia, SC

TheReinoldsGroup.com

The Reinolds Group
Columbia, South Carolina
TheReinoldsGroup.com

This book is dedicated to my loving bride, Rosalind Reinolds, who has never given up on me, George Bullard who has never stopped investing in me, Shane Stacey for always encouraging me to see the brighter way, The associational leaders whom I've had many of hours learning from and growing fond of as I watch them faithfully labor to care for the pastors and churches they serve.

Intro 9

- Know Thyself 16
- Consider New Ways 22
- Make Them Feel Understood 29
- Target Your Communication 38
- Be a Relationship Broker 45
- Build the Dance Floor 55
- Resource Guide 59
- Acknowledgments 83

About the Author 85

"The multi-vocational pastor movement is expanding rapidly. In Connect the Network to the New Normal, Chris Reinolds details the ways denominational and network leaders can engage this growing group of pastors. Read this practical book to understand how multi-vocational ministry is changing and what you can do to thrive in this new landscape."

-Sam Rainer, President of Church Answer, Co-Founder of Rainer Publishing, and President of Revitalize Network.

Read the book. Reinolds does a good job advocating about ministering more intentionally and effectively to multi-vocational pastors. Look forward to when this book comes out!

-Ray Gentry, President and CEO of the Southern Baptist Conference of Associational Leaders (SBCAL)

"Reinolds captured the feeling of surprise that network leaders feel regarding the shifts of the prior decade that provoked many network leaders to despair. This book is a wonderful read and very practical for networks."

-Chris Crain, Executive Director of Birmingham Metro Baptist Association

"I read through the book twice. It is insightful and practical. I look forward to using it in the coming months."

-John Thomas, Missions Strategist of Southeast Alabama Baptist Association

"Very VALUABLE read! It addresses our greatest dilemma as a network, with 40 churches out of 71 being multi-vocational. Very practical and doable steps to better relate and add value to this overlooked segment of Kingdom work."

-Jeff Knight, Lead Mission Strategist of Tuscaloosa County Baptist Association

In a time when churches are seeking clarity, Connect the Network to the New Normal gives simple steps for network leaders to help their churches lead into the future of the Church while also opening the door for timely conversations.

-Jarrod Spalding, Lead Navigator with Vision Partners

"I feel like often bivo work is presented as a disappointing but inevitable next stage in a secular world. Reinolds rightly points out that the focus of denominations is the full-time pastor with the bivo crew, not really serious players. This book reads really well for coaching denominational and network leaders in the bivo type of work."

-Andrew Hamilton, Author of The Future is Bivocational: Shaping Christian Leaders for a Post-Christian World

The future viability of church networks will be determined, in part, by how they support their bi-vocational, co-vocational, and multi-vocational ministers. Chris reminds us that this is not support for those 'lagging behind,' but empowerment of those at the tip of the spear of God's mission to reach our communities. This book is a practical look at how a network can immediately increase their connection to and support for this growing population of ministers.

-Jessie Cruickshank, Who-ology Founder and Author of Ordinary Discipleship: How God Wired Our Brain for the Adventure of Transformation

INTRO

Our family frequently took trips to Fernandina Beach when I was a kid. We only lived fifteen or twenty minutes away, and it was a cheap way to keep me entertained for hours. I vividly remember playing in the sand and making drip castles that would get smashed by the incoming waves. One time, I was standing on the edge of the surf, all of six years old at the time, waving to my mom, who was stretched out on her blue and white plastic folding chair with the metal teeth that would bite when you tried to close it. But as I stood there, I wasn't aware of what was happening behind me. Slowly but steadily, the tide rushed back to sea, building momentum, capacity, and girth. Before my mom could unstick herself from the plastic chair, before I could react to her terrified face, and before I could turn around, a massive four-foot wave (I was only 6) came crashing into my shoulders and driving me onto the sand–from standing happily to beach pancake in seconds.

It is my strong intuition that many of our networks and denominations are six-year-old me, recognizing something has shifted in our place in the world, noticing the changed look in the pastor's eyes, and not yet fully prepared for the wave to come. Specifically, that wave is the already building bi-vo and co-vocational ministry. Every day more full-time pastorates are floating out to sea, and multi-vocational ministers are hitting the beach with increasing ferocity.

Going off to Bible college and receiving your learning lumps at a small local church surrounding the school are quickly becoming days of the past. The average age of the senior pastor is climbing as fewer people enter the ministry out of high school, and seasoned leaders are holding on due to the financial inability to move into retirement. Author Tom Cheyney writes, "30 percent of Southern Baptist ministers are older than 55, while 10 percent are younger than 35. This alone could result in an approaching lack of pastors and church staff leaders within congregations nationwide."[1] In a 2019 study from the Religious Workforce Project, there was a "twenty percent shift between the percentage of Nazarene lead clergy between the ages of 35 and 54 years of age and clergy between the ages of 55 and 72." Pastors 34 to 54 decreased by 20 percentage points over almost 20 years."[2]

The reasons for this increasing number of multi-vocational emphases are vast. As church planters hit the scene fresh from training, many are intentionally volunteering to take on the role of dually employed because they see their place of work as a potential mission field where they have the opportunity to make everyday disciples—these individuals intentionally see themselves as "covocational". Brad Briscoe, in his book Covocational Church Planting, states that there is

---

[1] Harrison, R., Cheyney, T., Overstreet, D., Towns, E. L., & Stetzer, E. (2008). Spin-off churches: How one church successfully plants another. B & H Academic.

[2] "Nazarene Demo V.1 - Religious Workforce Project." *Religious Workforce Project* -, 9 Aug. 2021, https://religiousworkforce.com/nazarene-demo-v-1#percentage-lead-2019.

hope through their intentional living to set the example of what it means to make disciples of Jesus Christ in the places that they live, work, and play.[3]

Some leaders accept a multi-vocational role because the churches that call them have declined to the point that they can no longer afford a full-time traditional pastorate. Therefore, not necessarily voluntarily but rather out of necessity, these leaders are working in additional environments. Whether it is a secular field or an additional place in ministry, the mentality is that the additional work is simply a means to do ministry, therefore; in certain circumstances, these leaders see themselves as bi-vocational.

For greater ease of reading, I will, for the most part, refer to both bi-vocational and covocational leaders through the remainder of this book as multi-vocational. It is also imperative to note that multi-vocational ministers are not exclusive to the role of lead pastor, as there are an even greater number of staff persons within a church who work a multitude of jobs in order to supplant their income for the sake of pursuing ministerial endeavors.

For example, in the early nineties, the Christian Faith Baptist Church in Mullins, SC, employed several multi-vocational staff. The senior pastor, Glenn Ailshire, was the President of SoPakCo, a company that is one of the largest

---

3 Briscoe, Brad, Covocational Church Planting: Aligning Your Marketplace Calling & the Mission of God. Publisher. SEND Network. 2018

supplies of meals ready-to-eat (MREs) to the U.S. Military. During his tenure, they produced meals for latchkey kids who arrived home after school without a parent. The congregation was around 100-150 at the time but had six bi-vocational staff, including Glenn. The staffing structure, however, didn't inhibit their ability to do ministry it multiplied their capacity. The congregation and staff functioned in their ministry and programmatic emphasis as if they were three times larger. Therefore, limiting the scope of our definition of a multi-vocational leader to the role of lead pastor would, in fact, be myopic as many staff members function in a similar capacity.

Unfortunately, there is no place yet to quantify the significant impact of the multi-vocational ministry definitely, but what we know is that it is growing. As Rudy Gray points out in his article, the present statistics don't show the complete picture because so many churches are not turning in their annual means for record-keeping, and those that do, don't always check the "bi-vocational" box.[4] In the same article, Aaron Coe, CEO of Future City Now, observes: "A big part of the conversation we're trying to lead is that bi-vocational ministry is the new normal."

The new normal. If it is the new normal, why are we still struggling to develop an effective means to engage this new wave of normal ministry? From the hundreds of

---

4 Gray, R. (2016, November 3). *Is bivocational ministry the new normal?* Baptist Courier. Retrieved August 9, 2022, from https://baptistcourier.com/2016/11/bivocational-ministry-new-normal/

conversations I've had with denominational and network leaders across the country, there is a leadership vacuum that isn't being filled by seminaries, church leadership development pipelines, or denominational assessment processes. The reality is that the tide is shifting away from the traditional model of the ministry of the past 70 years, and if not careful, the network and denomination may be on the verge of getting pancaked.

More pastors, planters, replanters, and revitalization pastors are holding on to their 9-5, 10-3, and 2-12 jobs. Some have not only one job but three or four different side hustles to make ends meet. While I'm writing this e-book, I'm working four different jobs.

THE REALITY IS THAT THE TIDE IS SHIFTING AWAY FROM THE TRADITIONAL MODEL OF THE MINISTRY OF THE PAST 70 YEARS, AND IF NOT CAREFUL, THE NETWORK AND DENOMINATION MAY BE ON THE VERGE OF GETTING PANCAKED.

A common question from network leaders is navigating how to serve this growing group best. The reality is that this group isn't going to get any smaller; given the state of the church in North America, it's likely that these leaders will become the new model for ministry within the next ten years. Therefore it's all the more critical that network and denominational leaders begin to develop better ways to best engage with this group of leaders, lest they miss out on the opportunity and negatively affect the long-term sustainability of the local network and denomination.

In the following chapters, there are five ways network/ denominational leaders can begin to engage and build connections with multi-vocational pastors and their families. Formally, this book is written for network leaders and those who work on behalf of the network. But it is also a valuable resource for multi-vocational pastors, church staff members, and key lay leaders like deacons and personnel teams who can become a voice for changes to the associational, network, and denominational structure. It is also my hope to encourage multi-vocational pastors that network leaders are trying to overcome several challenges to add value to your lives and ministries. After seventy years of operating a certain way, shifting a paradigm takes time. Still, I assure you, multi-vocational church leaders, that many denominational leaders are laboring to do just that.

For the sake of simplicity, I am writing this book in a tone similar to Warren Wiersbe's writings, as if I were sitting across from you and talking like two old friends. These five ways are not meant to be the end-all-be-all of how to address this issue, its meant to be a catalytic starting point for the network and denominational teams to move from conversation to intentional action. What happens after that, I can only assume, well exceeds the content of this book. Thank you for trusting me with your time, I know how valuable it is, and I hope this little book helps you as you add value to the lives of others.

At the end of each chapter, you'll find a "Stake the Ground" section as an encouragement to start asking yourself questions about the current state of the network and adjustments that may need to be considered to utilize the information previously provided.

1.

KNOW THYSELF

"Essential intent applies to so much more than your job description or your company's mission statement; a true essential intent is one that guides your greater sense of purpose, and helps you chart your life's path." - Greg McKeown

Plainly asked, can you, as a leader, define what God has called the network to do and where he is leading the network to go in the next three to five years? Another question to consider is, what comes to mind when you think of a pastor? Do you picture an individual who visits church members, prepares for Sunday services, and occasionally attends network events, training, and lunches? If so, then you just pictured the minority of pastors in the world. Comparatively speaking, full-time pastorates are less frequent than multi-vocational ministers, and yet, most of our network efforts are geared toward the minority. Not only that, the network's mission is geared more toward the full-time minister.

In speaking with a rural network leader in Alabama (he's one of many that I've had this conversation with), he shared with me that out of forty churches in his network, only eight pastors were full-time. When asked if the thirty-two multi-vocational pastors were connected to the network in some meaningful way where he could bring value to them, he said, “No.” But quickly went on to talk about the success of their recent mission trips.

If the network's mission is unconsciously geared toward full-time ministers instead of ministers in general, you are missing a significant segment of your network. And if you cannot sufficiently answer the question of what God has called you to do and where he is leading the network in the next three to five years, then it is improbable that you'll be successful at connecting with this group of busy leaders. The number one way a network/denomination can better engage with multi-vocational pastors and leaders is by clearly articulating the network/denomination's mission and vision and retraining their thinking regarding what a minister in the twenty-first century looks like.

THE NUMBER ONE WAY A NETWORK CAN BETTER ENGAGE WITH MULTI-VOCATIONAL PASTORS AND LEADERS IS BY CLEARLY ARTICULATING ITS MISSION AND VISION.

These multi-vocational leaders have jobs to build relationships, families to lead, care and provide for, pastoral duties to shepherd, sermons to write, and leaders to train. They are juggling it all together because they feel a Holy calling to do more than they were doing before, and most are stepping into their future with decent clarity. If the network/ denomination doesn't have a similar clarity, then that leader won't likely invest the time and resources to invest in the status quo of a relatively unchanging network.

Denominational leader, these types of leaders need a clear direction and understanding of the future for their contextual family of churches. People want to be both inspired by what can be and informed about how we can get there together. When you talk about the collaborative impact of the network, does it inspire and encourage risk-taking, or does it simply drain energy? Does it leave prospective partners with a picture of a glorious future or a portrait of a broken-down dream?

In 1897, Ransom Eli Olds founded a company that would later become known as Oldsmobile. What began as a steam engine for yachts shop grew into a multi-billion dollar vehicle business that would revolutionize the automotive industry forever. In a stroke of genius, Ransom stopped doing things the way they'd always been done by switching the paradigm from making workers bring the parts to a location and started bringing the parts to the workers utilizing a wheeled platform. The assembly line was now in existence, and it changed everything.

Fast forward to the early '90s, and Oldsmobile was steady but struggling to keep up with the changing dynamics of a new market of buyers. Their name and brand wreaked of "Old" language and terminology. In an attempt to secure the next generation of drivers, they rolled out their new ad language, "This is not your father's Oldsmobile." As it turned out, it wasn't their customer's father's Oldsmobile because their existing market lost faith in the company by alienating them, and the new market either was content with daddy's Oldsmobile or wasn't convinced that a genuine transition was happening.

As the network leader, you're at a precipice moment in time in that you have a decreasing group that's sufficiently content with the status quo, a group that sees some value but recognizes a shift is needed, and a group that is disconnected entirely because the current mission and vision isn't engaging them in a meaningful way.

Widely known for its forty-year-old jingle, "The Best Part of Wakin' Up," Folgers, unlike Oldsmobile, is addressing the misconceptions about whom they are by owning what they've been, celebrating it, and still making progress into a new generation of caffeine addicts. In the summer of 2022, they released their radical ad campaign asking, "Are we your grandma's coffee? Yeah, we are, along with 34 million other coffee drinkers." At which time, the screen blips with scenes from busy moms, hipster twenties, business types, and robust families, all while featuring various brands in the Folgers line of products. They're finding success in celebrating who they are but acknowledging that they are already ahead of the perceptions from their past.

A great starting point for you regarding multi-vocational ministers, and the whole network, is first to have a clear, articulate, and meaningful mission **for today** and a vision **for tomorrow's** network kingdom impact that acknowledges who you are but also inspires others to be part of the tomorrow that you're already stepping into.

If you're a network leader, then you're likely familiar with how to develop a congregational life map that reveals the story of a local body of believers. But for many networks, they've never taken the time to develop their own life map. This can be a great way to begin identifying the unique thread that runs through the chapters of your network or denomination; thereby helping you to determine the next chapter of ministry; for a free guide to developing your network's life map, use the study guide at the back of this book or visit: ThePrismProcess.com/Resources

21

STAKE THE GROUND

- What language does the network/denomination presently have that is clear, meaningful, measurable, and impactful to describe its mission (today's objective) and vision (tomorrow's direction)?

- What will you begin doing today to prepare for the changing paradigm of vocational ministry?

- What will happen in the next 1-5 years if nothing changes?

2.

CONSIDER NEW WAYS

"Everyone thinks of changing the world, but no one thinks of changing himself." - Leo Tolstoy

It's crazy, but Patsy Cline caused some of my childhood memories to fall to pieces. In 1997, the downfall of a colossal empire began when Marc Randolph and Reed Hastings slipped a CD of Patsy Cline's greatest hits into a sleeved mailer and dropped it in a post office box. A few days later, the CD arrived undamaged by the US Postal Service, and Netflix was born. Thirteen years later, the movie distributor giant Blockbuster filed for bankruptcy. The world of accessing entertainment shifted because two guys decided to invest in a new way. Sweet dreams Blockbuster.

CHANGE WILL REQUIRE THE NETWORK TO TAKE A LEAP OF FINANCIAL FAITH.

Similarly, it may be time to reconsider how you're investing in pastors. A breakfast or lunch out is an excellent way to connect with a full-time church leader, but multi-vocational pastors are often pressed for time when it comes to day meals, and the leader and their spouse significantly protect evenings. This is a problem for most network/denominational leaders regarding their ability to build meaningful relationships with these leaders. Like a rip current, trying to fight back against it directly is even more problematic because you'll exhaust yourself and frustrate the leader you're attempting to connect with, often before you've had an opportunity to sit down for an initial conversation.

Therefore what's the solution? Well, what I'm about to suggest is one way that may help you make inroads and accomplish the other suggestions mentioned in this book. But it is going to require you and your leadership team to take a leap of faith in one of the most challenging areas for the majority of us–finances.

What would happen if you set aside specific dollar figures equal to two Sundays of pulpit supply per multi-vocational pastor in your network annually? I'll give you a minute to do the math. Now, what's it for? It's an investment from the network or denomination into an incredibly busy leader's mental, physical, emotional, and spiritual well-being. Suppose you arranged to have someone else fill the pulpit of this leader twice a year, beyond their standard vacation time, and paid that person(s) each week they filled a pulpit. If that could occur, there is the potential for a tremendous return on your initial financial investment because what most pastors need, especially multi-vocational pastors, is a break.

Not only is this an investment into the minister, but it is also an investment into their spouse, children, and church. When you're arranging and paying someone to speak for that multi-vocational leader twice a year, you're providing them a sabbath to just worship with their family or have a weekend break. This allows you, on the front end of a relationship, to create relational capital and credibility with this leader and their family, specifically their spouse. Since this leader frequently shares family time to do the work of ministry, the spouse and leader are not inclined to engage in other "after-hours" network opportunities unless they've already experienced the benefits of the network's investment.

Maybe finances are a significant factor for your network, and that large of a commitment isn't feasible, or perhaps you want to get something started now; what's the solution for you?

Another option is to consider working with some of your missionally vibrant churches in the region to see if they have capable lay leaders or staff who would be willing to volunteer one weekend a month to provide pulpit fill for these multi-vocational leaders. There might even be assistance that you could receive from larger state or regional entities that would provide stipends or personnel who also know the benefits of caring for the mental, physical, and emotional well-being of multi-vocational leaders.

In an association in north central region of Alabama, sixty-five percent of their one-hundred and eighty churches are pastored by multi-vocational ministers. Their Executive Director, has made a concentrated effort to assist these and other ministers with professional counseling for both themselves and their families during increased seasons of stress or when they simply need support.

For some smaller networks, there may be a benefit in leveraging the strength of a larger network/denomination in your relatively immediate area. An Executive Director of an association in the north central panhandle of Florida has developed a methodology called "The Association Simple" that they help implement within each association that joins their Florida panhandle associational network. In their framework, their model network assists sister associations by focusing on the work (mission) of the church instead of aiding the work (mission) of the Association. This allows those regional network leaders to remain autonomous but strategically align themselves better to strengthen the churches within their networks collectively rather than trying to maintain robust church supporting roles on a shrinking budget.

As it pertains directly to multi-vocational ministers, network leaders in the northeastern region of Florida are committed to ensuring pastors "Don't Pastor Alone," where they are intentionally include multi-vocational leaders. To accomplish this, they are purposely bringing in leaders who specialize in the nuances of multi-vocational ministry to speak directly to the needs of these types of pastors. They are frequently setting up a series of workshops at night for pastors who have to work during the day and are developing a digital framework for accessing training twenty-four hours a day and seven days a week.

Similarly, the executive director of a mega association of Southern Baptist Churches in California is finding success in providing live online training for multi-vocational ministers who cannot connect through the traditional means of network support.

In Tampa, with an urban and rural reach, there is one network that is platforming a micro church movement that has now reached 200 gatherings. Each neighborhood is viewed as a parish, and they desire to see a micro church in every neighborhood. One of the directors of the movement is a social entrepreneur that was frequently under-resourced as a traditional multi-vocational church planter. However, after twenty years, they decided to think outside the box and marrying ministry to social improvements such as serving underage youth, education opportunities, rehabilitation services, and scholarships for kids who cannot afford to pay for traditional education. Working with community partners, this multi-vocational pastor establishes relationships and waits for an opportunity for God to open the doors to share the gospel. In his words, “It doesn’t take long before someone asks, ‘Why do you care?’”

While your network may not be able to afford to go through such extravagant measures, it may be advantageous to look for network partnerships to leverage shared resources for the benefit of those ministers in your context.

These are not the only ways to invest in multi-vocational pastors in a way that significantly improves their personal lives, but they are great ways to start beyond simply asking the question, “What do you need?”.

(By the way, there were three different references to Pasty Cline songs in that first paragraph. I hope you got them...)

STAKE THE GROUND

- What percentage of your network investments are geared toward pastors and churches in traditional ministerial roles?

- Beyond the occasional Pastor's spouse Luncheon, how have you previously invested in a multi-vocational pastor's family?

- Who needs to be involved in the room to make the necessary shifts to change your investment strategy into multi-vocational pastors?

3.

MAKE THEM FEEL UNDERSTOOD

"I remind myself every morning: Nothing I say this day will teach me anything. So if I'm going to learn, I must do it by listening." - Larry King

It is a reality that people are interested in people that are interested in them. When someone walks away from interaction and feels like they were heard and considered, they want to repeat that experience again and again. There is a great temptation by most network and denominational leaders to share about the various processes and programs they can offer and why the network is valuable to the churches. Still, you are to avoid that at all costs. One of the best ways to help a multi-vocational leader (or any person) feel understood is to make them feel known and make them feel stronger.

MAKE THEM FEEL KNOWN

Time is a factor for everyone. Yet, as we've already mentioned, the co-vocational pastor's time is divided between family, work, pastoral ministry, preparation for the sermon, disciple-making relationships, and personal development; there isn't much time left for involvement with the network. However, given the recommendations of the last chapter, you will have likely bought the network at least one evening/weekend opportunity to connect with this multi-tasking minister relationally.

PEOPLE ARE INTERESTED IN PEOPLE THAT ARE INTERESTED IN THEM.

The key now is to not overdraft your credibility account. What I mean is that if the denominational or network leader can show themselves as an invaluable resource in their interactions with this minister, they will likely guard future opportunities to get together with them. When meeting with this leader, consider the following recommendations: Make It All About Them. Ok, so that's only one recommendation. This is a free book, so you shouldn't feel short-changed, but it really is the only one you need.

If you want to ensure the status of an invaluable member of their inner circle, keep the conversation focused on them. As a network leader, you are there to serve the churches and pastors in your region, and many times the best way to begin serving them is to stop talking and listen. Ask outstanding calibrated questions (which we'll get into in just a bit). Help the leader to know that they are heard by naming emotions ("sounds like that's something you're passionate about, frustrated by, interested in, etc."). Use language mirroring to draw out more information about a specific topic that you feel would help to understand their situation better (repeating keywords from their previous sentence in a curious tone: "some significant pressure... A background in engineering... the mountains of Colorado...). Summarize their situation using their own words so that you are affirming to them that you are intently listening.

The bottom line is to make sure that you keep the conversation tuned to radio station them. Resist the temptation to slip into advertising or problem-solving mode. By keeping the discussion focused on them, you are building up your credibility account as someone who cares for them and is genuinely interested in their story. Eventually, when they know you care, they'll make an ask, but until they do, keep digging. By keeping these interactions relatively short, (an hour to an hour and a half); and at manageable intervals (once every 3-4 months), you'll continue to convey respect for their time and the family time they are giving up.

MAKE THEM FEEL STRONGER

My friend and colleague, Jessie Cruickshank, Learning and Development Specialist and author of Ordinary Discipleship, frequently says, "Only another person can help you know what you almost know."[5] As the network leader, you are uniquely positioned to help others know what they almost know because you frequently understand the dynamics in not just one church but numerous churches in a specific region. You have the capacity to see the nuances of a particular segment of your network and how those differences connect and contribute to the cultural mentality of the region. You can frequently see patterns and themes in a church or region more clearly because you see the whole and not in part. Often, you have more excellent experiential knowledge of the ministry's work beyond the multi-vocational minister and, therefore, a deeper well of resources from which to pull information for practical application. This means that you, the network or denominational leader, can provide a broad perspective and ask specifically probing questions that help pull the minister forward.

Notice that I didn't say that the minister needs the right answers to the scenarios they are facing; instead, they need someone to ask them the correct questions to arrive at the necessary solutions for their context. This is helpful to multi-vocational ministers because they frequently need someone to help them know what they almost know. While providing a quick solution feels like the right thing to do in the moment, this stunts the individual's leadership capacity and makes them wholly dependent upon the network/denomination for answers. This type of hurtful help will likely prevent this leader from ever moving from a dependent learner relying

---

[5] Ordinary Discipleship: How God Wired Our Brain for the Adventure of Transformation, Jessica Cruickshank author, NavPress, published 2023.

upon the network to an independent leader generating for the greater good of the network.

HURTFUL HELP WILL PREVENT A LEADER FROM EVER MOVING FROM A DEPENDENT LEARNER RELYING UPON THE NETWORK TO AN INDEPENDENT LEADER GENERATING FOR THE GREATER GOOD OF THE NETWORK.

The ability to ask questions has always been important in building relational connections with others. Still, in our current circumstances, this has become a survival skill for a next-level leader. For the network to reorganize and prepare for the changing paradigm of full-time to multi-vocational ministers, we must be doggedly determined to invent or reinvent the type of work that's been done. None of this is possible without questions.

There is a multitude of resources that are out there about the power of asking better questions, and I'm not going to pretend I'm an expert. Still, I use the Telephoto Technique (Figure 3.1) when it comes to helping leaders who ask for an

Telephoto Technique

Wide Angle
What does a typical week look like for you? Where are you seeing vitality and vibrancy in your life/congregation? Where do you sense God is leading? What obstacles are you/the congregation facing? What would you do tomorrow if you knew you would succeed?
Frame the Subject
As you look at the landscape of the next year or two, what concerns you? What's (not who) the giant in the church that needs to be slain? What needs to be different for you/the congregation a year from now? What is the need in your community that isn't being addressed? When have you faced a similar situation?
Adjust the Focus
Earlier you mentioned ________, can you zoom in on that for a moment? Sounds like __________ is something that you're passionate about? Where did that (emotion) develop from in your life? What are you doing today that will lead to a different tomorrow? Summarize using their own words. Aim for "That's Right."
Snap the Picture
What will happen if nothing changes? Where will you be three years from now if you don't make this shift? If your friend were in this situation, what would you tell them to do? If God were to guarantee success, how would you proceed?

Figure 3.1

answer to a potential problem they're facing in their church. Start from a broad angle perspective and help them discern if this is a fruit issue, a branch issue, or a root issue. What assumptions might be being made for all sides? Is there anything missing from the situation that would be a quick fix? [6] Then begin to frame the subject of the issue by asking questions like, Why am I, or they, inclined to believe in this type of way? Then slowly adjust the focus to bring things into a clearer perspective. How could you look at this situation with fresh eyes? What advice would you give to a friend facing a similar problem? Is anyone jumping to conclusions? Has all the information been made clear? What would the person on the other side of the table be inclined to think is true? What if the opposite was true?

These questions are probing questions designed to dig directly into the heart of a particular issue and help the leader think around the problem to see a probable solution. Generally speaking, leading questions should scan the surface for pieces of information. As the mental lens finds its target, use a calibrated question like “How or What” to frame the subject clearly into the circumstance. Then adjust the focus to isolate the pain points for the pastor by summarizing their situation with their words and naming their emotions to the point that you can get them to respond with “That’s right.”

Finally, when you’ve discovered the source of the issue, snap the picture, or in the words of Frank Bettger,, explode dynamite with a question like, “If nothing changes, what will happen within the next year?[7] In the words of Regina Dugan,

---

[6] Berger, Warren. “The Book of Beautiful Questions: The Powerful Questions That Will Help You Decide, Create, Connect and Lead.” Scribd.

[7] Bettger, Frank. “How I Raised Myself From Failure To Success In Selling (Chpt 8).” Touchstone. Kindle Edition.

"What would you try if you knew you could not fail?"[8]Have you prepared your family, leadership team, church or yourself for that? By saying "yes" to allowing this to continue, what are you saying "no" to?"

In many cases, it is helpful to a leader if you can connect a similar situation from the past to their present situation and share with them how it was resolved and its long-term effects. If sufficient information has been provided and the questions properly probed, the leader will feel more inclined to move toward a particular action. If there are specific resources or expertise that the network has that may assist them, provide that information to them as an open invitation.

By asking questions, you've made the multi-vocational pastor feel as if they've been heard and helped them brainstorm specific solutions from within their decision-making abilities. They now will likely see you as someone who desires to strengthen them rather than someone who makes them feel inferior because they couldn't solve the problem on their own, even if they take you up on the offer of outside assistance.

---

[8] Dugan, R. (n.d.). *From Mach-20 glider to Hummingbird Drone*. Regina Dugan: From mach-20 glider to hummingbird drone | TED Talk. Retrieved August 9, 2022, from https://www.ted.com/talks/regina_dugan_from_mach_20_glider_to_hummingbird_drone/transcript?language=en

STAKE THE GROUND

- Who else within the network/denomination is capable of engaging in these types of conversations to spread the responsibility over a broader range of people? Can you provide them with a per diem?

- Before the meeting, create a list of calibrated questions (How or What) as prompts to keep the conversation going. Spend time practicing naming emotions and mirroring language in a curious tone.

- What are you often thinking about when listening to a pastor? Try not to think about anything other than the words coming out of their mouths.

4.

TARGET YOUR COMMUNICATION

"The single biggest problem in communication is the illusion that it has taken place." - George Bernard Shaw

When most of us receive an email, we usually decide in less than a second whether or not we're going to read or respond. In fact, at this present moment, I have five-thousand four hundred and fifty-nine unread emails in my inboxes. I understand that this is likely to cause many of you anxiety, but if it makes you feel better, most of it is junk mail–probably. Regardless, multi-vocational leaders need the facts pertinent to them. Most networks are still operating on the assumption that people will, like a gold-panner, sift through the details to find the information that is gold to them–this isn't true. If the relevant information doesn't readily rise to the top of the pile, then the busy pastor, and most people, will move on and mentally classify future potential information as inapplicable to them. I mean, why do you think this book is so short?

Multi-vocational ministers need someone who will provide them with relevant information and allow them to make the necessary decision about their involvement in a moment. Inundating a co-vocational leader with superfluous information will often cause them to stop reading your content, undermining your attempts for the network to be a viable voice in their life. While the widely used Microsoft Word created and clip art-laden network newsletter may be a fun information easter egg hunt for some, it's simply additional noise in an overly noisy world.

THE WORD-CREATED AND CLIP ART-LADEN NETWORK NEWSLETTER MAY BE A FUN INFORMATIONAL EASTER EGG HUNT FOR SOME, BUT FOR OTHERS, IT'S SIMPLY ADDITIONAL NOISE IN AN OVERLY NOISY WORLD.

To get information across to the multi-vocational leaders in your network, you need to craft that information specifically for them. While I understand that this sounds like additional work, the reality is that you're reading this book to understand better how to serve these types of ministers. A simple tool is to open an excel spreadsheet with six columns and list out the full-time and multi-vocational pastors, their churches, and email addresses (See Example Below). A more high-tech but equally free option is to utilize MailChimp to create various email "Lists" that separate your multi-vocational ministers from your full-time pastors.

Church	Full-Time Pastor	Email	Church	Multi-Vocational Pastor	Email

Organize your emails to bi-vocational leaders with the information most relevant to them at the top and the things they are not likely to engage in. However, you still want to provide an invitation at the bottom. Consider bullet point titles with one-sentence explanations underneath. If you have multiple information points at the top of your message, avoid clickbait tactics to have them read more because this will ultimately undermine your desire for them to read the entire message since it pulls them away from your email and to another site. If you need a decision, consider sending a separate message geared to that specific topic. Make it personal to them. Studies have shown that an email that directly addresses a person by name gets higher open rates (I don't have a source. Take my word for it.). Finally, informational emails are more than sufficient once a month for the multi-vocational minister.

However, email isn't the only means for communicating in this day and age. There are lots of mediums for Networks and Denominations who are looking to increase communication and collaboration between themselves and among their multi-vocational ministers.

One avenue is to use your existing network's Facebook Page as a platform for communicating with these busy leaders. This doesn't mean that you are to increase the frequency of your postings and hashtag them #multivocational. Instead, you can create individual Group pages that are directly linked to your Network's Facebook Page. By creating a group, you can add or invite multi-vocational ministers to a group that is specifically going to have items relevant to them posted in it.

Another option is to create a Network only Slack Channel. For little to no cost whatsoever, you can create a texting-based forum where multi-vocational leaders can share stories, encouragements, ideas, pictures, and struggles free from the concern of those outside their circle seeing them. This would give them a place to interact with one another for strength and support immediately.

As a reminder, the content you provide for multi-vocational leaders doesn't always need to be digested by them. In the Four Square Network, over eighty percent of their pastors are multi-vocational. This reality shouldn't be perceived as a negative as many of these leaders are covocational by choice. They are intelligent, hard-working, and multi-tasking leaders who benefit from the quick resources they can provide to a busy team of lay leaders.

As a network leader, part of your digital communication strategy could simply be to provide curated content from existing churches within your context or faith tribe that has

Communication Reminders

Be Creative
There has never been an easier way to be creative without having to be creative. Online services like Canva, Pixlr, and Unsplash remove all excuses about not being able to produce professional grade communication.
Be Aware of Customization
If you want to get your message across then you need to tailor it to those you wish to reach. Make sure to use information that is relevant to the reader and always be sure to include their name in the body of the message.
Be Consistent
A key part of communicating through online mediums is that you have to be consistent. Whether its once a week or once a month make sure you are readily reaching out to the multi-vocational minister as a reminder that you've not forgotten them.
Be Content Relevant
Make sure that what ever information is going out is meaningful to the reader whom you are sending it to. Don't feel like you have to draft the Magna Carta with every message you send. A personally tailored text message has more meaning than a mass email or general Facebook post.

Figure 4.1

been templated to fit several different circumstances. For example, employment contracts, background check forms, employee evaluation forms, generic rental agreements, and promotional material are all resources that you can curate in a single location from some of your leading churches and provide it to a multi-vocational leader so that they can forward it to the appropriate people when it is needed.

Another valuable digital resource you can provide is reviews of teaching and learning materials. Time is a factor for all leaders, and if you or someone in your network would be willing to provide an executive summary of the content you're consuming with the main ideas and illustrations, it can help the busy leader grasp and utilize new concepts that they otherwise may miss out on.

Regardless of how you're connecting, use Figure 4.1 as a guide for communication.

For some, you may be reading this and deciding if there is relevant information to put at the top of your next network message. The subsequent chapters will assist you in developing some of that content, but in the meantime, take a cue from chapter 2. Consider writing a personal email to each multi-vocational minister to schedule their first "rest weekend." Use a Jotform or Google Doc that allows specific dates to be chosen and marked as "claimed." Most of those forms will allow you to limit the number of responses for a particular date, preventing it from being chosen again.

STAKE THE GROUND

- What percentage of communication is relevant for a multi-vocational pastor?

- What is the tone of the message that are sent from your network/denomination? Are you expressing humble service, or are you encouraging active participation?

- Whom do you need to have a conversation with about making changes to your communications processes?

5.

BE A RELATIONSHIP BROKER

That is the great joy of being chosen: the discovery that others are chosen as well. In the house of God there are many mansions. There is a place for everyone - a unique, special place. Once we deeply trust that we ourselves are precious in God's eyes, we are able to recognize the preciousness of others and their unique places in God's heart." - Henri J.M. Nouwen

Craig Tuck, Executive Director with the Charleston Baptist Network, has made it their mission to be a relationship hub for pastors and churches in their network. They don't view themselves as the experts; rather, they see themselves as the broker to the experts in their context. Whether full-time or multi-vocational, you, as the network leader, can function as a convener of people in at least four different ways to assist the pastors and churches in your context.

FINANCIAL PARTNERSHIPS

While financial stability may be one of the components for the multi-vocational pastor working several jobs, it doesn't alleviate the stress of providing for his family and his church body. Feeding a family is expensive. Feeding a family and engaging others in meaningful relationships to build disciple-making relationships is even more costly– and the cost to go out to a restaurant is an even higher expense. Leaders who step into ministry while maintaining their secular role are likely creative entrepreneurs who know how to get things done with excellence and make the most out of a little.

Because of the continued financial pressure point in their life and ministry, these financial frustrations can lead to frustrations within the ministry or, if not guarded well, in the home.

YOU ARE UNIQUELY POSITIONED TO ENCOURAGE AND COACH THESE MULTI-JOB MINISTERS TO SEE CONNECTIONS THAT POTENTIALLY MARRY MINISTRY AND MONETARY NEEDS

While most people are familiar with the names of the tech giants who brought us the iPhone, MacBooks, and Apple Watches, many are unfamiliar with the name who is partly responsible for introducing those giants–Bill Fernandez. Fernandez, a friend who attended Cupertino Junior High with Steve Jobs, the Apple visionary, lived on the same block as

Steve Wozniak, the Apple programming guru.[9] One evening, a simple walk around the block allowed Fernandez to introduce Jobs to Wozniak, and a technical revolution was born.

As a network leader, you are uniquely positioned to encourage and coach these multi-job ministers to see connections that potentially marry ministry and monetary needs and, thus, possibly, begin a gospel revolution. In most circumstances, you may know various non-profit organizations that need forward-thinking leaders. You're likely connected to, or have long-standing relationships with, business leaders in the area and can provide recommendations for trustworthy team players. In some circumstances, you may see an opportunity to convene two individuals who have the capacity to go into business with one another for the mutual benefit of the multi-vocational leader and the missional opportunity the new business could create.[10]

In his book, Next Wave: Discovering the 21st Century Church, Steve Pike emphasizes the need for at least five different funding streams for a multi-vocational pastored

---

[9] Eadicicco, L. (2014, December 8). *One of Apple's earliest employees describes the first time Steve Jobs met his genius cofounder Steve Wozniak*. Business Insider. Retrieved August 8, 2022, from https://www.businessinsider.com/how-steve-jobs-met-steve-wozniak-2014-12

[10] Gruidl and Markley. "Entrepreneuerships as a Community Development Strategy." 279

church to remain viable.[11] The traditional tithes and offerings stream primarily teaches the congregation the importance of faithful stewardship of their God-given resources. Funding from donors outside of the church that provides resources from monetary to non-monetary items such as chairs, tables, coffee makers, and other items allows the congregation to function in a welcoming environment. The third recommendation for revenue is the multi-vocational pastors' primary income role. In some cases, both spouses will have to take a role in earning income in the changing landscape of ministry. Another revenue stream for the church is the non-profit partnerships built within the community context. If a homeschool group is looking for a place to meet, a girl-scout troop needs a place for their regular gathering, or a school is looking for a location to house their end-of-year events, these are all potential revenue streams for the church to consider for sustainability. Lastly, the multi-vocational pastor may benefit from developing a for-profit partnership with the community by meeting a practical or felt need–from running a second-hand store, to a hair salon, to a dance studio. There are many options to consider to assist these multi-vocational ministers.

As a network and denominational leader, there is a way to connect struggling pastors to financial solutions that allow them to do what God has called them to do both in the context of the church and as parents and spouses. Knowing what those various options are and helping a multi-vocational

---

[11] Steve Pike: "Next Wave: Discovering the 21st Century Church." ArtSpeak Creative. 2020. Excerpt Scribd.

minister explore those possibilities is another way that the network can better connect with this growing group of leaders. In fact, some networks and denominations are moving to a ministry model where they hire contractors from within the network who can learn skills or leverage skills they already have to advance the kingdom endeavors of the network itself; these people may well be multi-vocational ministers.

RELATIONSHIPS

As a bi-vocational pastor, I'm always seeking more knowledge. It doesn't matter how much I read, listen to, download, podcast, or consume; I can never get enough knowledge. Since I'm doing most of my ministry in various capacities, I always feel like I'm playing catch up in the information race. Everyone is always asking me, "Have you read this book? Have you listened to this podcast? Have you watched this documentary?" There's just so much, and the reality is that most of it doesn't significantly contribute to my life in a meaningful way.

However, there is a connection to knowledge that a network or denominational leader can provide that is invaluable–a connection to others. There are precisely two types of connections that you, as a network leader, can help with: Willing Mentors and Sharpening Peers.

MENTORING RELATIONSHIPS

A willing mentor is worth their weight in gold. A mentor can make people better players, workers, students, family members–and ultimately, better people.[12] In his book, Focus: The Hidden Driver of Excellence, Daniel Goleman points out that a mentor's influence energizes because it helps set clear expectations, encourages because the mentored feels heard, accelerates decision making because someone is helping them think through things, and makes life more enjoyable because someone is celebrating the wins and mourning the losses with them.[13]

The difficulty for the multi-vocational minister is finding the time to find a mentor that would work for them. Let's be honest with one another; some people simply don't mix well together. An easy-going "get there when I get there" personality type doesn't fit with an "early is 15-minutes before the event" personality. However, you are in the ideal role to assess the personalities of a potential mentor and mentee and evaluate the benefits of a possible connection. The other reality is that this mentor doesn't have to be a pastor; it could be someone who is a well-respected Christian business leader interested in investing in someone else. You can evaluate, assess, and then connect these two persons, which

---

12 Tony Dungy. "The Mentor Leader: Secrets to Building People and Teams That Win Consistently". Scribd.

13 Goleman, Daniel. "Focus: The Hidden Driver of Excellence." HarperCollins Publishers. Scribd.

can tremendously impact the life and ministry of the multi-vocational minister.

PEER RELATIONSHIPS

The other type of connection a denominational leader can convene is the sharpening peer. Life in ministry is lonely. It's lonely for the pastor, it's lonely for his wife, and it's lonesome for his kids. Stepping into a multi-vocational role puts the pastor in the position of always "being on."

When a pastor and his family are perpetually engaged in a culture of separation and isolation from peers, this isn't biblical nor spiritually healthy. Without peers around them to encourage and challenge them, there will be a progressive hardening of the heart (Hebrews 3:12-13) which can lead to destruction in their lives.[14]

However, the ministry is far less lonely and much healthier when there are peers, especially ones with a similar family dynamic. As the network leader, you already know those in the family of churches who are in similar situations. By creating a space for the convening of pastors and their families to interact, you open up the opportunity to release a pressure valve that doesn't have the chance to release all too often.

---

[14] Tripp, Paul David. "Dangerous Calling." Crossway Publishing. Scribd.

WHEN A PASTOR AND HIS FAMILY ARE PERPETUALLY ENGAGED IN A CULTURE OF SEPARATION AND ISOLATION FROM PEERS, THIS ISN'T BIBLICAL NOR SPIRITUALLY HEALTHY

It may be wise for the network or denomination to invest in a few leadership/skills assessments for the pastors in your region if it hasn't already. Not only would this be beneficial for them, but it would also allow you to create a database on the general skills, abilities, and natural inclinations of the leaders in your network.

MINISTRY RELATIONSHIPS

When I was younger, I used to help on a dairy farm, and by help, that means I used to ride around on four-wheelers pretending to do something meaningful. Regardless, in my mind, whether it was real or not, I cannot definitively say there was a steel silo that would store items to prevent outside forces from destroying them. While those types of silos are useful, church silos are not. A multi-vocational minister is perpetually battling the competition mindset in their church and in the churches in their immediate geography.

A family of churches should function as a collaborative force to impact lostness in the world. Still, far too often, they operate as competitive aquariums attempting to lure the fish from one bowl to another. The multi-vocational pastor can easily get caught up in the net of this sort of behavior. However, your role as network leader allows you the opportunity to be Switzerland and provide insight into long-term partnership opportunities between the multi-vocational and vibrant churches in their immediate area.

Imagine the collective benefits of non-territorial churches working together to help advance the message of Jesus in gospel deserts. The assisting church provides operational and structural support to outreach opportunities, while the multi-vocational pastor and parishioners focus on building relational connections to their community context. These long-term partnerships significantly reduce the stress and people power necessary to do the work of ministry in their context, thus reducing the strain on the multi-vocational pastor, their family, and their leadership.

You likely have the relational capacity to connect these sorts of mutually beneficial long-term partnerships successfully. These relationships strengthen the individual pastors and their congregations and increase the legitimacy of the church's claim to be the one body of Christ–thus functioning as a testimony to the watching world.

STAKE THE GROUND

- List out the community and business leaders you know or with whom have a connection. Consider if there are possible connections that you can make between these two groups for the mutual benefit of the other.

- How could you create contractor positions who work for the network/denomination from among the multi-vocational pastor? What skills/abilities do you presently need better to serve the cloud of churches in your context?

- What sort of system does the network possess that allows inventories to be made on pastors' leadership/ strength assessments? What needs to be done to change this?

- How can you begin to connect churches around a central need in their community context?

BUILD THE DANCE FLOOR

Leader, the reality of your present situation isn't lost on me. You're dealing with shrinking budgets, struggling churches, disengaged pastors, and potentially a growing value gap between the network/denomination and the churches you're called to serve. Add to that dynamic the elements that are taking place culturally, politically, denominationally, and nationally, and you have a virtual dumpster fire, and all you have is a water pistol.

But here is something that you have that no other group has, relational proximity. You have the ability to function as a faith family member to the churches in your geographic area. Your gift is that you can reach out and touch the leaders and churches in your area of service. You can put your arm around them when they are at their wit's end. You can comfort them at the sudden loss of a loved leader. You can encourage them like no one else because you are near to them and know them.

The other benefit is that you have the opportunity to pull these leaders together and develop a shared vision of where God is leading them as a faith family. Their geographic and cultural dynamics are unlike any other group anywhere else because they are serving in a regional area, and God has fit that set of churches together to accomplish something far greater than any one of them could accomplish on their own.

While you may not be able to implement each of the recommendations in this book immediately, here's an idea: start choosing the planks of wood you want to set down for multi-vocational ministers each year. What's one thing you can do over this next year that can be a plank of wood for them? Choose one or two new planks each year, and you'll have created a little floor over the next three to five years. Over the next five to seven years, you'll have completed a little platform. Before you know it, you'll have built a network dance floor where multi-vocational ministers feel both celebrated and cared for.

TAKE WHAT HAS BEEN LEARNED THROUGH THESE PAGES, AND MAKE IT BETTER

I hope that reading these pages has challenged your thinking about what could be for the future of the network in your context. I sincerely hope that you take what has been learned through these pages, make it better, and apply it to your context. Develop more and better ideas than I could imagine and share them with others so that this growing group of multi-vocational pastors are served well regardless of the dynamics of their situation.

Multi-Vocational Investment Options

Pastoral
Quarterly Coaching Sessions w/ Network/Denominational Liason Mentorship Opportunities w/ Missionally Healthy Church Pastors or Christian Business Leaders Partnerships w/ Sister Associations for additional resources Connecting long-term partnership opportunities between churches
Personal
Association pays and finds pulpit supply for 1 to 2 Sundays off per year outside of existing vacation days. Peer Group Family Fellowship Opportunities Connecting financial opportunities that match the pastor's natural skills
Educational
Evening Workshops around Specialty Skills Digital Framework for Accessing Online Training Live Online Evening Training Certification Program through a local Seminary/University
Soul - Care
Free Counseling Options for Pastors and Family Bringing in speakers who specialize in the nuances and struggles of multi-vocational ministry Creating space for leaders to develop meaningful relationships

If you'd like more information or to discuss how to transform the paradigm of your current context, we'd love to hear from you and set up a conversation. Feel free to reach out to us at ThePrismProcess.com because we love helping churches and denominational leaders imagine their network through a whole new light.

RESOURCE GUIDE

SECTION 1.0 - KNOW THYSELF

As an associational, network, or denominational team, spend some discussing what comes to your mind when you think about the pastors that you support in your network. Then complete the Check the Facts Exercise below.

Check the Facts Exercise

	Full-Time	Multi-Vocational
Percentage of Pastors		
Percentage of Staff (Including Pastors)		
Percentage of Staff (Including Pastors) 10 Years Ago		
Percentage of Network/ Denominational Budget From Full-Time vs. Multi-Vocational Churches		
Percentage of Network/ Denominational Resources (Time, Money, People, Events)		

- What did the information from the Check the Facts Exercise reveal about the current state of your association, network, or denomination?

- What surprised you about the differences between the amount of resources for full-time vs. multi-vocational churches?

- Based on the full-time to multi-vocational status changes of the last ten years, what is the projection of multi-vocational leaders in the next seven to ten years?

- What current resources have the capacity to adapt to a multi-vocational focus?

- Who in your network could you leverage to strengthen the connections to the multi-vocational staff?

SECTION 1.1 - KNOW THYSELF

Everyone loves a good story, whether it is the clattering sound of an old wizard traveling into the land of Hobbits, the thumping sound of a helicopter's rotors just before landing in a hot zone, or the epic call for a team of heroes to assemble; everyone loves a good story. Every good story has heroes and villains, moments of triumph and tragedy, and feelings of elation and heartbreak.

The same is true of the story of your network. Do you know the story of your network? It may not seem that important, but here is a truth to ponder: An uninterpreted story can hinder your future, while an interpreted story can fuel your future.

Does your team know your network's story? Do they know how to tell that story? This short course will help you create a visual life map that identifies the critical hinge moments of the life of the network in a way that creates creative chaptering.

Purpose

At some point in time, the cloud of churches within a given region determined that they had a collective need to be served in a specific way, this is the point where your network (box) was birthed. At the point of origin, the churches and the network were in a virtuous cycle in that the network served the churches, and the churches funded the cloud. However, as time goes by, the needs of the churches and the focus of the network can drift into places that no one expected.[15]

Principle

Therefore, since we also have such a large cloud of witnesses surrounding us, let us lay aside every hindrance and the sin that so easily ensnares us. Let us run with endurance the race that lies before us, keeping our eyes on Jesus, the pioneer and perfecter of our faith. - Hebrews 12:1-2

After having given an exposition of the chapters of the faithfulness of God's people, the author of Hebrews appeals to his readers to press forward into the future that Jesus has laid before them.

Similarly, your network must be expositionally examined to take note of the chapters of its existence. Simply put, in order to look ahead, we first benefit from looking back. The purpose of looking back is not to reclaim the "glory days" but rather to understand where we came from and how we got to where we are today. All through scripture, God calls his people to "remember" but never calls them to nostalgia.

Understanding and interpreting our past can help you step with wisdom and understanding into your future. Now is the opportune time to grow from where you are and avoid trying to grow back into what you were before.

---

15 The Life Map is a tool created by the founders of Younique, helping people interpret their personal stories. It has been adapted to help church and network teams interpret their organizational story.

How it Works

Divide your Leadership Team into groups of 3-4 to brainstorm the top 5 high points and top 5 hard times of the network's history. As you list each of these high points and hard times, you should try and identify the year they occurred. Write down the date your network started. Focus on the hinge moments where the direction of the network was impacted the most.

- **High Point Examples:** New Leader, New Initiative, New Growth, New Church Added, New Church Plant, First Annual Meeting
- **Hard Times Examples:** Failed Initiatives, Competing Forces, Lack of Team, Lack of Resources Conflicts, Outside Challenges, Changes in the City/Country/Denomination

As you add them to the list rate on a scale of +1 - +10 on how it was a "high" point. Then rate on a scale of -1 - -10 on how it was a "hard" time. Report out each group's top 5 high points and top 5 hard times on a flip chart using two columns and combine until you have at least 10 points each. Use tally marks to identify repeated hinge moments.

As a group score each of the ten hinge moments on a scale of 1 to 10, positive or negative, depending on if it's a high point or a hard time. Always be sure to record the year of the hinge moment.

High Points
1845 - 7 Churches formed the network 1945 - First Executive Director hired +3 1964 - Local Campground Purchased +10 1981 - Network merged with sister network +7 1985 - New regional name was approved +6 1990 - Church planting initiative began +5 1994 - New Building Purchased +9 1997 - 30 new church plants celebrated 1999 - Seminary Extension Program +9 2006 - Sold Building & Invested Money +10 2008 - First Multi-Cultural Church-Plant +8 2010 - Missionary Training Center +5 2014 - Revisioning of Network 2017 - Restructured to Ministry Teams 2021 - New Executive Director Hired

Hard Times
1907 - 10 Churches Burned in City Riot 1943 - 60% Network loss due to war -9 1959 - Executive Director was murdered -7 1967 - Loss of funding due to doctrinal disagreement about the war -7 1971 - Executive Director fired 1977 - Executive Director Role made P/T -5 1983 - Doctrinal Clarity Issues -10 1987 - Largest Network Support Dried Up -9 1998 - National Network Crisis -4 2004 - Network office vandalized -10 2007 - Doctrinal Disagreements on Race in network 2011 - Lowest engagement of network participation -6 2013 - Long-term Executive Director Retired -4 2017 - Younger Leaders Disinterested in network participation

FORCE CLARITY: TAKE FIVE MINUTES AS A GROUP TO CIRCLE THE TOP 10 NETWORK LIFE MOMENTS FROM EITHER LIST

High Points
1981 - Network merged with sister network 1990 - Church planting initiative began 2006 - Sold Building & Invested Money 2008 - First Multi-Cultural Church Plant 2014 - Revisioning of Network
Hard Times
1971 - Executive Director fired for Cause 1987 - Largest Network Support Dried Up 1998 - National Network Crisis 2007 - Doctrinal Disagreements on Race in network 2017 - Younger Leaders Disinterested in Network Participation

Map the top 10 hinge moments on the Life Map.

- Use the color red to plot the average yearly worship attendance of churches in an association over the timeline.
- Use the color green to plot the community's population growth within the association's borders.
- Use the color blue to represent the number of baptisms reported annually (if known).
- Put a star where new point leader stepped into leadership.
- Another line couple be used to track budget

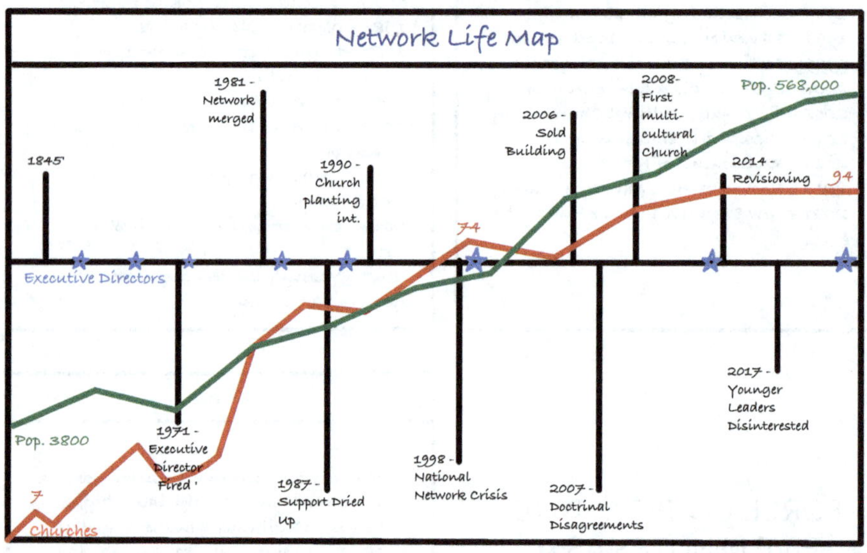

Create "Chapter Divisions" Across The Life Map

- Work with the team to create "chapter divisions", no more than five chapters total. Draw chapter breaks where a significant shift in direction took place.
- Work with the team to create chapter titles for the top of the life map.

-Work to have the chapters "Tell a Story", meaning they relate in some way to one another. Keep the chapter titles to 2-5 words.

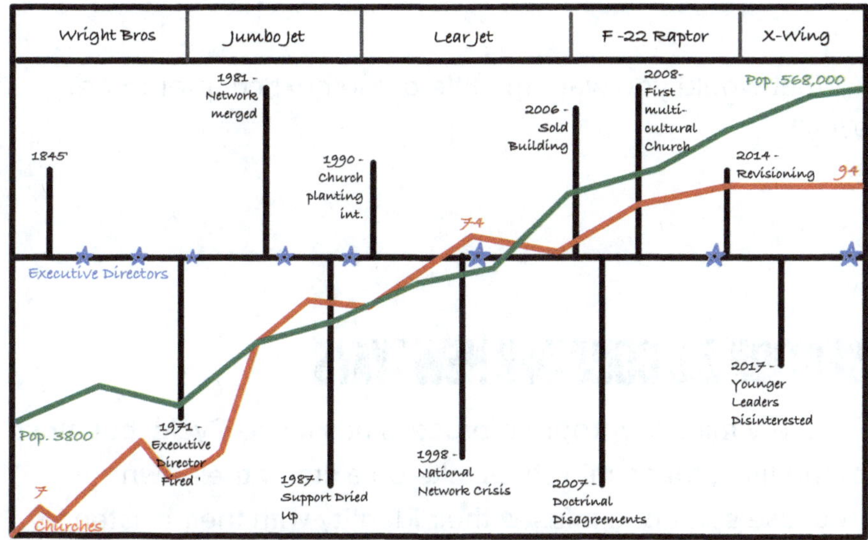

-Invite the team to step back and identify 5-10 specific insights they see and any essential learnings.

-What patterns do they see?

-What stands out as they hear the stories around each of the chapters?

- During any particular chapter, what was the network known for?

- What would you want the title of the next chapter to be? Why?

SECTION 2.0 CONSIDER NEW WAYS

Every ministry/program/process has a Life Cycle, but most of the time, these ministries take on a life of their own because someone infuses their identity with their existence. We can tend to continue keeping ineffective ministries running far longer than necessary and lose opportunities to see traction or resources diverted to other places. By saying "Yes" to allowing an ineffective ministry to continue, you may be saying "No" to a potential new opportunity for the network, association, or denomination.

Place all the Network's current ministry offerings on the Life Cycle bell curve. Indicate the year it started and # of full-time vs. multi-vocational pastors currently engaged in it annually.[16]

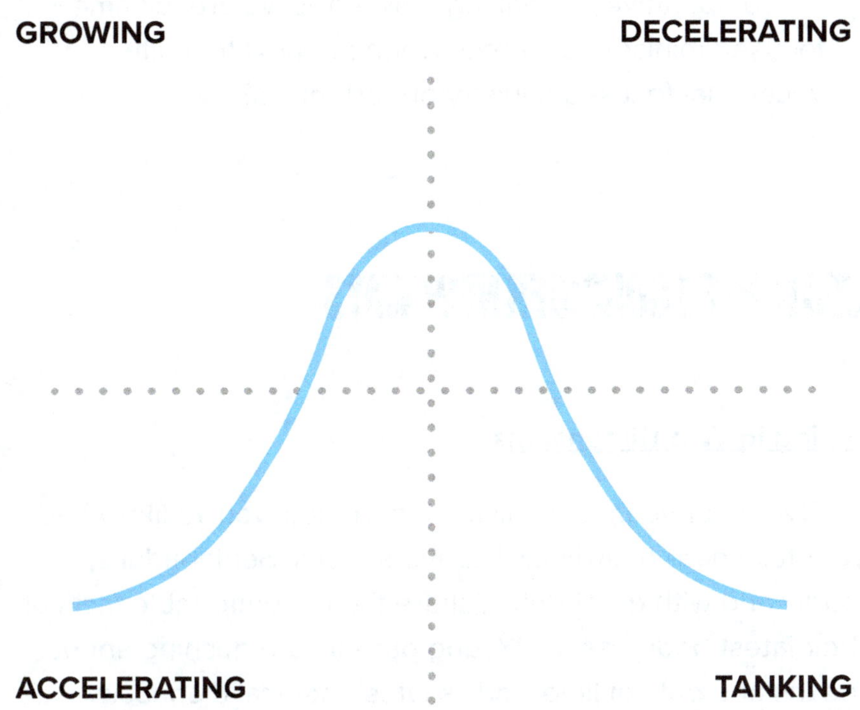

- Considering the financial contributions of the full-time vs. multi-vocational church in Section 1.0, are there ministries that the denomination needs adapt to be more versatile?

---

[16] The Language of the Life Cycle Quadrant Analysis originated with Tom Paterson

- What programs or resources could be caged in order to invest more in multi-vocational ministers?

- Comparatively speaking, how effective are full-time focused ministry resources when put next to multi-vocational focused ministry opportunities?

SECTION 2.1 CONSIDER NEW WAYS

Giving in Two Dimensions

Over your years of ministry experience, you've likely had your fair share of awkward conversations. Senior adults, loudly and with great detail, share the uncomfortable facts of their latest bodily issues. Young parents are gushing about the ins and outs of little Darla's latest medical diagnosis. Parents and teenagers spill the details of their dysfunctional relationships as you gain a glimpse inside the lives of people you thought you knew. But there is one topic of conversation that, at first blush, presents as the third rail of ministry: Money.

If you want to guarantee a low attendance Sunday, let the congregation know that you'll be teaching on Biblical Stewardship of our God-Given Resources the following week. Regardless of how people feel about it, financial stewardship and its subsequent patterns are an additional character in the narrative of a congregation.

To borrow the illustrative model of John Bunyan's Pilgrim's Progress, in every congregation, some characters comprise the narrative of how the story of that congregation plays out. If the unity was portrayed as a weak older woman, you know that strife, division, and gossip will be firm friends gathered in the foyer. If truth is the primary protagonist, then you can be sure that deception will always be lingering in the shadows to assail any who dare to venture too far from the center.

In the same way, stewardship is an actor that reveals much about the congregational characters as a whole. Remember that Jesus clarified that "where your treasure is, there your heart will also be (Matthew 6:21)."

As a network leader, you can look at financial stewardship and the patterns it creates in two dimensions: What It reveals about the Church and what it Reveals about the value of the Network to the church.

What it Reveals about the Church

The stewardship lens is one of the initial lenses that you can use to assess a church. When considering sitting down with a church to evaluate their possible next steps toward meaningful progress, the church's giving trends over the last five years can, at times, provide perspective on the strengths and roadblocks the congregation may be encountering as they look to the future. As a denominational leader, you may already have access to this data from annual reporting mechanisms. But, even a few simple questions can be revealing, such as: Over the last five to seven years, has the financial giving of the congregation trended up, down, plateaued, or been sporadic? Why do you think that is? What does it reveal about the state of the church? These trends can function as smoke signals that, if followed through additional questions, can lead to a source of health that can fuel the future or challenges that may hinder future progress.

10 YEAR ANNUAL GIVING TRENDS

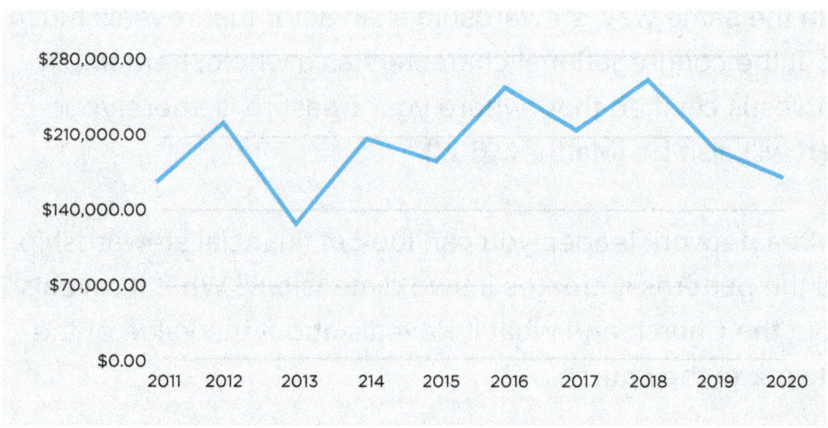

Consider the information in the figure above; what questions may it raise? For me, it would cause me to ask questions like do they have a clear sense of knowing what God has called them to accomplish together, is it apparent that there is unity among the church body or are they filled with conflict that causes some people to hold back funds regularly until they get their way?

The critical insight into the financial trends of the church is not a question of strategy and practice but rather a question of stewardship and surrender: Is this church surrendering to the Lordship of Jesus in all areas of their lives, including finances? As a caveat, there are sometimes unicorn financial situations within the context of a church, such as a bookkeeper's error where the church was 10k short of what their reports indicated. Most of the time, though, as a network leader, you can discern at least three certain realities from a congregation's financial faithfulness pattern: Vision Clarity, Collective Unity, and Spiritual Vitality.

Vision Clarity

When a church has a clear vision of the future that God is pulling them, they align its resources to achieve that vision. Such alignment can indicate that the congregation owns and embraces the trajectory of where God is taking them; therefore, there is a more significant reason for them to support that vision financially. When a congregation feels like they are part of a vision that brings them closer to God, there is a greater likelihood that they will financially support that vision out of the joy of playing a part in what God is doing and the benefit it will be for others.

However, if there is no clear vision of the future story God is writing amid a congregation, then people's support will only extend as far as their perceived temporal needs are being met. This creates a "get by giving" financial situation that may indicate the church is functioning in a maintenance mode. This type of scenario is hard for any pastor or leader to navigate for long-term future viability and growth.

Collective Unity

If a congregation isn't unified, the individual financial contributions become alms for rewarding or deserts for punishing. In the absence of unity, the individual parts that make up the whole congregation base their giving on their individual felt needs or preferences. Stewardship of resources isn't about contributing to the health of the whole; instead, it can be focused on keeping the status quo of the content few.

A congregation who are collectively unified in their mission of what God has called them to do generously display that through their financial stewardship. The individuals who comprise the whole church body see that their financial investment into the work benefits those they serve and love. A people who are unified wholly give willingly for the benefit of the whole.

Spiritual Vitality

An additional factor for a network leader to consider is that the financial trends of a congregation reveal the spiritual vitality of the disciples being developed in the context of the church. Suppose a congregation has a healthy programmatic emphasis, plenty of activities for various generations, and several staff to ensure that the church's activities keep functioning. Still, the financial trajectory over the long term grows stagnant because spiritual maturity, dependence on

God, and authentic sacrificial worship is absent. In that case, this likely reveals a breakdown in the church's disciple-making effectiveness or spiritual vitality.

A church concerned about the whole development of the body of Christ sets the model for the disciple as to how Jesus would live if he had our family, job, kids, spouse, neighbors, and finances. When a congregation embraces this idea of discipleship in its context, stewardship of our God-given resources becomes a non-negotiable. This type of church will see a steady increase in financial stability over the long term as long as it focuses on the biblical development of the whole person.

Trends Spur Questions

The bottom line is that financial trends do not necessarily reveal the whole picture of a congregational circumstance. But they do unearth questions based on their overall trajectory. Use the following grid to consider the types of questions you could ask a church based on their financial trajectory.

What it Reveals About the Value of the Network

While the financial patterns within a specific congregation communicate various narratives in its particular bubble, the financial patterns of the contributions to a network have a much broader story. When the individuals who make up the church contribute to the work of the ministry in their local congregation, they do so because they see a relatively immediate return on that financial investment: Services are

GIVING TRENDS	UP	PLATEAUED	DOWN
Vision Clarity	Do they have a clear understanding of the Future Vision into which God is pulling the congregation? Is it clearly communicated regularly in their structure?	Is the congregation confused about the direction in which they should step into the future? Are there many opinions on how to proceed but no clear consensus? Are high capacity leaders frustrated?	At this stage, does the congregation feel the burden of maintenance more than the breath of the Messiah? Have they likely replaced vision with management processes?
Collective Unity	Does the congregation display high trust and open communication between their peers and leadership? Do they see stewardship as an opportunity to help advance the church's mission as they pursue God's vision for their future?	Within the church, is there a high level of appreciation for those who continue to serve within the four walls of the church? Is there a reduced tendency to look for ways to impact their community because of a belief that they "must make themselves ready" to receive those from the outside?	Are the relationships within the congregation nominal and surface level? Do people know each other by name, but don't display collective unity concerning the future other than they want it to look similar to the "recent" past?
Spiritual Vitality	Is this congregation empowered by a spiritual vitality that is deep and meaningful? Does worship extend into the members' lives and beyond the building's four walls? Are most members aware that they are growing steadily into a greater likeness of Christ in their existing context?	Does the congregation have pockets of people who faithfully attending and seeking to grow as fully developed followers of Jesus? Are the majority of the members simply checking the box on their religious duties and then go about their lives?	Is the congregation largely comprised of individuals who do not consider spirit aliveness as anything they need to concern themselves with? Will the church likely remain content sitting in their same pews and singing their same songs? Is the word "Vitality" likely to upset the status quo?

weekly, the staff is active, programs are functioning, and the ministry is happening.

However, when the network leader evaluates the financial contribution of individual churches to the network itself, that communicates something else entirely. It may indicate whether or not the church believes that the network can do something beyond what the church can accomplish on its own. Specifically, the second dimension of the giving analysis for the denominational leader can be an indicator of the perceived value of the network to the church.

and the level of confidence they may or may not have in whether the network will be able to help them get to where they are trying to go as a church.

Indicator of Value

One of the number one questions a network leader is asked in today's religious culture is, "What value does the network bring to our church?" Suppose a church isn't financially or is minimally contributing to the network. In that case, it is an indicator that either the church or the pastor doesn't see the benefits of investing financially into the work of the local/regional network. There are a few reasons that they may have this perception.

1. They believe that the network cannot provide something new or innovative to help them advance the mission in their context.

2. They possess a different perspective on how the network should deliver value to the local church/pastors. Therefore, the church puts its potential investment resources in other places of greater interest where they have agreement or alignment.

3. The church perceives the network as a resource center whose sole objective is to work with struggling or failing churches in their context.

Regardless, a lack of financial investment in the network indicates that the perceived value proposition of what the network does or offers is low.

However, a network that is capable of communicating the value that it brings to churches, in particular, will, in most cases, see a steady or increased financial investment. This will likely occur because the local body of believers, through their pastor and leadership, see the benefits of their network's engagement.

Next Step Insights

It's important to note that in some networks, the root cause of a decreased investment from the local church couple simply be a decreased giving within the bodies of believers. A reduced financial investment from the body will inevitably affect the other organizations dependent upon the local church further down the line.

But this is why the network or denominational leader must have a healthy fundamental understanding of how to flash assess a church's finances. As a reminder, the network or denomination exists to serve the churches in a way they cannot typically serve themselves.

An individual pastor or church may be feeling the pressure of reduced financial provisions due to internal congregational pressures, there may be an economic depression in the region due to cultural and socioeconomic shifts, or there may be a combination of certain situations that are coming together in a single moment in time.

The network leader who can recognize these trends and tendencies can better assist churches in taking a next step. Some churches' financial struggles reveal that they are in need of making meaningful progress by entering into a period of prayer. Others may reveal that a spiritual awakening needs to happen in their midst. Still, others may need a collective realignment of where God will lead them in their next season.

In some cases, a pattern of increased financial contributions may reveal an opportunity for collective work among congregations that can take place in a community to alleviate financial pressures. The network leader may be able to connect an economically depressed region of churches with a financially stable congregation from another part of town to advance the gospel mission of them all.

The network or denominational leader that adds this giving lens to their bag of resources that they bring to a network of congregations is in a position to bring more excellent value to those whom they serve, thus potentially advancing the growth of the local church and raising the perceived value of the local network.

- What does the financial contribution from the multi-vocational church reveal about the value of the network?

- What questions should you be asking to the multi-vocational church leader whose financial markers are plateauing, growing, or declining?

- Are there financial patterns in your network that reveal an opportunity that maybe has gone unseen?

SECTION 3.0 MAKE THEM FEEL UNDERSTOOD

Tools for Improving Your Conversational Mining Techniques adapted from Christopher Voss, Founder of The Black Swan Group.

Sample Calibrated Questions

- How is that worthwhile?
- What's the biggest challenge you're facing right now?
- How does this fit into what your objectives are?
- How does that affect things?
- What's the core issue here?
- What are you trying to accomplish?

Sample Emotional Labels

- It sounds like ________ is important to you.
- It seems like you value__________.

- It sounds like you don't prefer _________.
- It seems like _________makes it more tolerable for you.
- It seems like you're hesitant to _________.

Tools for Brainstorming and Decision Making adapted from Tom Paterson's Four Helpful Lists

What Works	What Doesn't Work	What's Confused	What's Missing?

SECTION 4.0 TARGET COMMUNICATION

As a potential resource for targeted communication, the network or denomination can provide or connect multi-vocational teams with a database curated from various locations that will assist them in practical ways. Use the form below to build a resource database that links directly to source files that will assist the multi-vocational leader.

Title	Description	Source	Contact Person/Link

SECTION 5.0 BE A RELATIONSHIP BROKER

Tools for Assessments and Building Healthy Teams and Making Healthy Connections

- APEST
  - APEST is a ministry assessment emerging from the most comprehensive statement of ministry structure, that of Ephesians 4:7,11-12. Each one of us grace has been given as Christ apportioned It is he who gave some to be apostles, some to be prophets, some to be evangelists, and some to be shepherds and teachers, to prepare God's people for works of service, so that the body of Christ may be built up.

- CliftonStrengths
  - Stop wondering what you're good at. Start knowing with Gallup assessments. Our assessments identify your natural talents, so you can perform better in your job, build stronger relationships and achieve personal growth. Gallup assessments are easy to take, and your results are instantly available.

- DISC
  - DiSC® is a personal assessment tool used by more than one million people every year to help improve teamwork, communication, and productivity in the workplace.

- Enneagram
  - The Enneagram is a system of personality typing that describes patterns in how people interpret the world and manage their emotions. The Enneagram describes nine personality types and maps each of these types on a nine-pointed diagram which helps to illustrate how the types relate to one another.

ACKNOWLEDGMENTS

Huge thank you to the following people who allowed me to pick their brains and provide insight as real-life practitioners who are pioneering new ways as I was writing this book:

Chris Crain, Executive Director of Birmingham Metro Baptist Association

Bob Bumgarner, Executive Director of First Coast Churches

Brian Nall, Executive Director Pensacola Baptist Association

Mike Stewart, Executive Director of Missions at Great Commission Association of Southern Baptist Churches

Jarrod Spalding, Lead Navigator with Vision Partners

Jessie Cruickshank, Learning & Development Specialist with Proved Expertise in Organizational Psychology

Sammy Ortiz, Founder of Community Collective · Underground Network - Entrepreneurial Ecosystem Builder in Underestimated Communities· Door Opener

PRISM PROCESS FOR ASSOCIATIONS/NETWORKS/DENOMINATIONS

Every church in a network is moving into a future of unlimited possibilities. While not all of these possibilities are the ideal outcome for a given body, there is still an opportunity for continued kingdom impact. The pastors that make up these churches are looking for network and denominational leaders who can deliver value to the churches where they are presently and help them to see a new way forward.

The problem is that most denominations/networks are operating on an incremental paradynamic model that stopped working forty years ago. What's needed today is the development of vibrant strategies to catalyze the gospel movements necessary in your context. We can help. **Visit: ThePrismProcess.com/networks**

PRISM JOURNEY FOR CHURCHES

Our dream is to see churches empowered on a congregational journey that is both spiritual and strategic in nature. Your church is uniquely fit together by God to fulfill His divine purposes in your context. We desire to see your congregation moving toward fulfilling the Kingdom potential that is part of God's redemptive plan. Imagine what could happen in your community if your church began being pulled forward by God's future story of ministry for them as a congregation on mission. As your church lived into its Future Story of Missional Ministry as a congregational movement, you would see families restored, relationships mended, communities made whole, and eternal kingdom impact for years to come. **Visit: ThePrismProcess.com/church**

ABOUT THE AUTHOR

After serving on ministry teams across the Southeastern United States, within his local association, and alongside some of the leading consultants in the country in denominational and network ministry, the call to help bring greater clarity and value to network leaders became impossible for him to ignore. Chris loves to help conscientious leaders create strategic solutions for future growth; he wants to see them thrive in their personal, church, and network lives. For more information, visit ReinoldsGroup.com

www.ingramcontent.com/pod-product-compliance
Lightning Source LLC
LaVergne TN
LVHW052009160826
845678LV00005B/1699

* 9 7 9 8 3 5 1 5 0 6 7 0 8 *